# Born to Electrify

Poems by: Raquel Reyes-Lopez

Raquel Reyes-Lopez's poems are electric eels and chain lightning woven into winter scarves that you just want to wrap yourself in...There is crackling power here—just as Edison gave the light bulb, Raquel, with her debut chapbook, *Born to Electrify,* gives us all a necessary gift that glows and hums.
—Eric Morago, *What We Ache For*

Raquel Reyes-Lopez shows us a brave woman, honestly and confidently sharing pain and beauty in a matter-of-fact way. Even when the truth is hidden between angels and hummingbirds, eyelashes, life and death, it is there. With no apologies. Raquel has, as in the last lines of "Mujer de Hielo Autopsia" state: "a line of poetry/ sequenced/ into her/ DNA."
—Tobi Cogswell, Co-Publisher, *San Pedro River Review*

Raquel Reyes-Lopez's poetry gives our inner-child a voice to tell us where it hurts most. We long to take her in our arms and comfort her. But, she is too strong for that. She is the voice of the healed who returned to absolve our guilt. Her desire to redeem us makes us feel worthy, again. Read Raquel Reyes-Lopez and you will feel your deepest wounds begin to mend.
—Raundi Kai Moore-Kondo, *Let the Ends Spill Over Your Lips*

© 2014 Raquel Reyes-Lopez
Published by Sadie Girl Press
SadieGirlPress@gmail.com
Cover art by Esmeralda Villalobos
Author portrait by Fernando Gallegos

# Table of Contents

*In memory of 9/25/2012 & 5/4/2014*
*may you both be the stars that guide me*

# Born to Electrify

*Chasing and catching the rays of the sun,*
sit on a constellation, and take one last look
at Mars. Observe the fall of Europa and wait...
because R.I.P. means rebirth in progress.

When you're ready, baby, BLAST
like a heat wave CRASH
underneath the Northern Lights
with a BANG.

You'll be raised in Alaska
by your Wiccan mother;
she'll teach you to love

> the Earth
> meditation
> using herbs
> invoking elemental spirits.

You'll be everything you tried to be
but couldn't.

Take this second opportunity.
Remember the steps your new mother will teach you.
I'll tell you of them now.

### 1

Realize the power is within you.
You're 70% water with traces of phosphorous.
Your creator made you a natural conductor.

## 2

Shock people—
you were born to electrify!

## 3

Find a woman whose beauty
far exceeds Jupiter's rings. Here's a hint.
She exists once every hundred years.
Her personality will shapeshift
from swan, to wolf, to butterfly.

## 4

In all you do make sure it's for love.
Live, wait, and die in the name of love.

## 5

Walk into the light without fear.
Enter life as we know it with a BANG.
Bring joy into the room
with your innovated body's
first newborn cry.

# New Dawn

These tears are blood, the unease of menarche.
Feet swing from the toilet, coping with agony.
Conflict arises. I do as the dying do,
outstretched hands into air, asking God
to forgive me of all sin.

I call out for my mother. She rushes in.
My lips quiver. I tell her with a dry mouth
too afraid to say goodbye,

> "I can't stop the bleeding.
> I am dying."

She looks down at my underwear
and approaches me with Messiah's smile.
"My daughter, you will live," she says.
I glance at my savior, my creator
see her with newborn eyes
for the first time thankful.

# With Hunger

Jesus asked me to present to him the person I love most.
I showed him my mother. I told him how she's playing
God's substitute while God is gone.

I told Jesus how my mother broke loaves of bread,
fed me and the dogs. How there were some nights
we only had fluids as food. Not to nourish but to fool
our stomachs into believing they weren't empty.

I started telling Jesus how my mother's strength
tastes bitter from the sacrifice of minimum wage shifts.
How old age weighs her shoulders down quickly.

I confessed to him
when mother fed me
a spoonful of her strength
I hid sugar cubes
under my tongue.

Remembered Mary Poppins' song while holding back tears
*A spoonful of sugar helps the medicine go down*
*the medicine go down, the medicine go down.*

Jesus laughed. I raised my hand and silenced him.
I told him to pray to my mother, beg her not to stop
believing in God. I explained to him it's blind faith
that's keeping her alive.

He became silent. I looked at Jesus one last time. While walking away from him I hoped he believed in me enough that I would one day have the strength to tell my mother God's not here...yet.

# Honey, I left your tongue on the kitchen counter.

I found it under our mattress. You might want to rinse off the dust bunnies sprinkled on it. That's if you want to start talking again.

Next time, please don't ask our child if she's seen it.
I don't want to start involving her in our problems.
She's only four. I would have helped.
All you had to do was ask.

Honey, it's back-to-school night, on my way there
I found your finger, and wedding band. She didn't
notice when I picked them up from the sidewalk.
I give up trying to work things out for you.

Her teachers showed me all her drawings.
She's always drawing me, her, and little bear.
You're never in the pictures with us. Although
she does say she has a dad, except he's always busy.

Honey, I tried to carry our child in my arms back home.
It wasn't a long walk. She's so small and weightless.
I thought you were going to meet us at church. I guess
you forgot. She didn't complain but she asked for you.

I didn't know what to say. I suggested to her I could call
for a cab. She said she didn't mind walking and asked
to be put down. She's five now and wants a new box
of crayons.

# Mother, let me be your lamb.

Mother's dirt earth eyes brought me security as a child.
They would blink softly, blow soap-and-water bubbles.
The kind I made with my lips once.
Then they would vanish, like magic.

Her glossy coal curls sunk me in like dirt in water.
Every day she made me believe the joy blooming
within me was immortal. Then she would smile.
Her smile would bake infinite mud pies in my heart.

My mother would do this trick. She would make
my soul wobble and jiggle the same way children
giggle while shaking Jell-O.

I was her awkward child. I followed her rules,
never whined, or cried. I always stood by her side.
Mary's little lamb.

Things have changed. I am no longer a child.
She's forty-eight now, no longer twenty-nine,
and I've been a stray these past seven months.

Her liver spots have expanded to her neck,
shoulders, and they will keep on growing.
The doctors say her blood is starving.

Mother's body pleads but she won't eat.
She takes her fragile hands, aching bones,
and sharp pains as God's will.

Mother, let me be your lamb again.

Dictate words onto me that sting
and burn like a false messiah
claiming liberation is suicide.

Go on and believe by killing
the innocence of your lamb
God will answer a prayer.

# As Long as Organs Let Us

Within the closet hangs
the silhouette of woman.

Gowns that will accent childbearing hips,
drape over lovely breasts, and cling
onto every curve.

Underneath clothing is the example
of how hungry man's desire
for her will be.

With every diet, she will hope
the material kisses every inch
of her skin right.

The gowns are a test
to see if she is the shape
to lust for and chase.

Mirrors are the answer
to whether she will pass or fail.

Beauty is trademark.

Like those lifeless threads hanging
worthless on wooden hangers.
Cup breast, hug waist, and slap
ass as if size matters.

I'll introduce you to beauty.
Just show me your liver,
lungs, and pancreas.

We will all run as fast and live
as long as our organs let us.

# Mujer de Hielo Autopsia

*"Her heart thrilled to Mitochondria."*
– Hideaki Sena, Parasite Eve

Thin butterfly antennae eyelashes blink.
Perfect coal curls drop down. Miniature
dandelion parachutes. Her mud earth eyes
shine hope. She sends wishes to the future.

One day her hair, blood, and bones
will be discovered by scientists.
She'll get funding for DNA
reconstruction.

Her seventeen years of life
were damaged by pesticides,
GMO foods, and color dyes.

Mad men       wearing
              white gloves
              white coats
              would G A S P.

They'll see how at eighteen
she differed from her species.
As well as the years that followed.
She fortified and replenished
her genetics with minerals.

She had high amounts of plant blood.
Chlorophyll constantly cleansed
her kidney of toxins. Part of the reason
she lived to be 200.

Scientists will peek at her through lenses.
Drooling, they'll whisper among each other

>*Oh so lovely, oh so beautiful, so healthy.*
>*What a shame we couldn't have met her organs*
>*to save her mitochondria.*

They'd stop. Gorilla glue every bone
into its appropriate socket. Filling
her face with clay to get a model
of what she looked like alive.
She was 5'6, slender, but curvy.

They'd OO-OOO-AAA-AAA
amongst each other, overtaken
by ape-like instincts. Wishing
they could have bred with her.

Upon completing her
with the wrong color eyes,
one of the scientists
would notice

through his microscope
what the others missed:
>a line of poetry
>sequenced
>into her
>DNA.

# Unwelcomed Thievery

smack attack
moist lush lips
press and push
press and push
honey coats
into tongue
layer
after
layer
rumble-ready punching
angry bees swarm
buzz-buzz-buzzing
into frontal lobe

knee caps generate
pre-seismic activity
aftershocks follow
6.0 H magnitude quake
eyes open and flash
        crimson
        rosy heat steams
        off cheeks
        first kiss
        stolen

# Geocaching

Two pink auras burn in darkness.
Moans echo, waiting for discovery.

Bodies are foreign countries
wanting to be washed
by the perfect passion
pressure.

Continents from neck, hips,
and inner thighs need hands
to rush down waterfalls.

A thirsty body doesn't crave
a gentle touch. It will demand
aggressive force
consistent multiple

boom

Boom

BOOMS

explosions bringing life
back to drought land.

Push roughly into flesh.
I want to feel a BANG.

Make my garnet eyes
sparkle.

Rattle.

Wring out
the long overdue
earthquake
and shake
with me.

# Passerby

He says my eye color is off. I don't say a word.
I know it's a drunken slip slurred. He begins
to siphon out the brown in them.

I want to stop him but I let him keep viewing me
through a set of past life eyes. His fingers brush
skin and paint her jawline on my face.

I watch his pupils dilate. They're stuck in spring.
He whispers, "You look beau...kind of like her."
Now, I understand my place. I am summer

and my body a transition for him to jump
into autumn. These bones are his carrier
this flesh just a rough draft to his voyage.

# After the Break Up

I walk nude. Breasts bounce.
Nipples perk from chill.
I close the door behind.
Open tattered shower curtains.

I pull up from inside the drain
hairs. The only thing you left
behind. I slap them against the wall.

You tossed my love into the sewer
as easy as your bowels push shit.

I can only wonder
if I grab a wire hanger
use your hairs as bait
fish within the drain
could I reel
my heart
back in?

# Measuring

6:00 AM

I am up against the doorframe.
With a pink Sharpie I stain wood.
I slowly measure progress.

I keep an eye on self-love's intervals
watching them spike and randomly stop.

7:00 AM

My ribs pull apart
lungs short of breath.
I am having
an asthma attack
remembering him.

7:45 AM

I am tempted to go back to
unnatural desires and plan ways
for him to want me.

7:55 AM

Darkness.

8:00 AM

I remember the photographs
sent to all those other women.

8:15 AM

I drink my coffee black
eat half an orange scone.
Today self-love measures
taller than my 5'5 frame.

# No Era La Misma de Antes

Mother you don't need to understand
the language he broke me in.
Embrace me, wipe my tears,
rub my back until this sorrow
falls back to sleep with me.

How did you get rid of the pain,
the loss your first love gave?

*"Cuando me fui ya no era la misma de antes,"*
she says sweetly.

Mother you have eternal love.

Would you cut open your stomach
and let me crawl back inside?
I need nine months of your nurture
to mend myself whole again.

# Amor en el Pueblo

He romances Socorro during soft June rains.
Drops hit her aluminum rooftop making smooth
splashes of rushed in soul.

Passion sizzles off their skin. A red aura blooms.
Sweet serene discussion begins.

*"Mi amor yo te adoro. Vine a cantar te las mañanitas,"*
he says to her kissing her forehead gently.
He strums his guitar. The air fills with tune.

Singing echoes throughout *el barrio*. Everyone hears
him declare his love to her with *canto*.

Heaven smiles down at the couple. Rain continues.
It pours down harder, blessing *el pueblo*, relieving
their land from drought.

For once the townspeople whisper truthful *chisme*.
"*Amor nace milagros*, love births miracles. *La virgen*
made sure there will be harvest for us all."

Crashing into pavements, the rain sounds off
a rounding applause, and says farewell.

*El sol sale* Socorro kisses him as the last
chords of the song are strummed.
Tears swell *en sus ojos de alegría*.

# Master Baker

He knows how to whisk seduction.
The only special ingredients required
are parts of him.

He stirs into a bowl a cracked egg,
a cup of flour, and sugar. Slowly
he adds his eyelashes, his finger,
and a piece of his tongue.
He is that committed.

We wait for the oven
to preheat to 375 degrees.
The temperature and awkwardness
in the kitchen become unbearable.

He's baking cookies for Etelvina.
He hopes she'll take a bite out of them
and distinguish every part of him
he reserved for her.

Soon she'll feel his hands heating her
into a flawless tender crisp. He'll eat off
parts of her she never knew existed.

He'll hold her and make promises.
She'll believe them all because his kisses
melt into Aurora Borealis.

Then she'll experience his authentic
one night stand flavor. The aftertaste
left on tongue come morning
when he's gone.

The oven beeps. Preheating is done.
He gently places the cookie sheets inside.
He tells me when he talks to her
his eyelashes fall when he blinks.
He's never been that nervous before.

That's when I realize
when we kissed
not a single
eyelash
fell.

# Why his apology never reached my ears.

His lips inch across kitchen floor tiles. I am full
of brown-eyed indifference. His arms are glued
onto the ceiling fan. They whirl around wildly;
sometimes his hands try to reach down
for my throat.

In an empty saltshaker I put all his eyelashes—
the ones I ripped off.  Preserving his eyes into
a sweet strawberry jam isn't a romantic thing
to do. But it spreads easily across my burnt toast.

When I get lonely I lug around his torso
like a teddy bear. I have him sit down
with me for dinner.

I know he's upset with me part of the reason
he hardly likes to talk. I shouldn't have thrown
his cookies in the trash.

This morning I snipped off my ears &
tossed them into the fish bowl. I couldn't stand
hearing him cry out her name.

# Fracture

Think of me
when purple clouds pull a-part
by the winds of your changing heart.

Then view a world                    glinting with gold
and dream of me                      in emerald hues

           colliding
           against
           lunar
           tears.

# Putting Away Groceries Barefoot

My sighs liquid lava pools
toasting ojos de miel
hasta que sean cecina.

Hands cup breasts.
My name circulates
in his pupils.

God hides
between eyelashes
too embarrassed
to watch us.

I grab onto shoulders
as my neck is sucked;
conversation spills.

"Have you ever held
a baby hummingbird?

It feels the same
as holding you,
*frágil*," he says.

His compliment
stuffs huesos huecos
soothing joint pain.

He places
a strawberry
in my mouth
gently

without guilt
I devour.

If our toes
don't keep
a distance
& touch

I will fall
in love
with him.

Si eso sucede le voy explicar
que gracias a las cenizas
de sus besos aprendí
a no negar la muerte.

# Los Pajaritos Cantan

Hummingbirds hang on telephone wires
wanting to fly again, stuck waiting.
Sun rays beat up my delicate skin.
All I recall is his dirt dipped eyes.

Before he left we kissed
     y todas las flores
     se hicieron
     marchitas.

& Earth was left thirsty
but the moon she melted
into my pupils.

# Warp Speed

We kiss. Cracking ribs.
Lungs birth out galaxies,
our tongues push them
upward and exchange
a foreign universe.

We saliva swap the Cosmos.
Our eyes open. We realize
there is much within
each other to discover.

Excitement pops.
Two auras magnify.
He is a scorching blue.
I am luminescent purple.

Hands tremble. Breath
becomes hot and heavy.
It is
      fall
        i
          n
            g

              in love
              for the first time
              again.

# For Aldehyde

There's a half sheet of blank paper crumbled
in your father's pocket. I got a pen in my purse
somewhere. That's if I haven't lost it.

April came. Two lines revealed you were mine.
Your father twirled me in the kitchen.
As the eggs fried we discussed
whether you would be a girl
or a boy. I felt complete.

I was whole with you inside of me.
One afternoon at the prick of a needle
a fractured dream landed heavy on sand.

> hCG 70,000
> hCG 13,352
> a week passed
> hCG 9,000
> and another
> hCG...0

My body is a hormonal tidal wave in flux.
Aldehyde, I'm trying to breach the barriers
of a shore where we're not allowed to touch
to say good-bye.

I know I am not alone in this.
I look at the moon teary-eyed.

In the freckles of the Cosmos
a communal hymn is ringing
for us who have lost.

# Everyone is having a good time and I'm stuck here at Walmart.

The woman in the bathroom stall next to mine is sobbing.
I hear her shuffling through her purse, hands scurrying
in panic, and then *thud*.

I glance down at my feet and see a positive pregnancy test.
Her sobbing stops, she is silent, but the sniffles give her fear
away. I kick the test back to her.

I watch her hands shake as she reaches down to pick it up.
Her cell phone rings and she answers, "Hello."
I hear a man's voice yelling at her.

She leans her head against the stall *thud, thud,* and *thud*.
She takes a deep breath and lets it out slowly.
"No, it was positive," she says.

Her cell phone hits the floor, the battery pops out,
and her screen breaks. She wails, "But I don't
want this thing inside of me either."

I feel her shame steam off the thin stall's walls.
I can't help but think what I wouldn't give up
       to be pregnant again,
       to have never miscarried,
       and how life is so unfair.

# A Confession for Father

I said goodbye on Walnut Street
7,600 + 55 tears fell
onto pavement

as far as God is concerned
I am still there          waiting

for a heart defibrillator
to bring me back to life.

# How to Drink the Moon

Don't ask for forgiveness. It's better to show
remorse with distance. Now with a straw slurp
up the Moon. Darkness is home.

Ask God when the Sun reaches him to tell him
you will never return and beg for his pain
to be gentle.

Then pray to the universe with your absence
the one in love with you will share
solitude with stars.

# Resonance

Everything dies after birth.
Look! The sun is burning out.
You're crying   too soon, fool.

Do you not see the moon

q
u
i
v
e
r
i
n
g
?

She and I will be gone.
The universe will leave you
an orphan.

# Ethereal Outline

Acknowledge he's in the night sky. Grab scissors.
Open bedroom window and climb up to rooftop.
Begin cutting the Heavens. Ignore God's yelling

*Mortal do not rip him away from where he belongs.*

Smile widely as you set him free.
Wake up feeling accomplished.
Remember him        alive.

# When decades pass by they will dig a grave in your mouth.

Do not confuse this for a fly,
or be disgusted with time.
Just think of it as gum.

Will it really take seven
years to digest this?

Just chew
with back
teeth and
swallow.

Go back to simple memories first.
Remember when you baked mud pies
under the sun and fed your mother for days.

Go on, break the raven's wings,
and watch as the gods smile.

# Solitude and Memories

Mother, I saw your face in the freckles
of my bedroom wall. Moonbeams
don't warm me but this silence does.

I remember your eyes broken honey
combs, and *tu miel* dripping out
of pupils when you missed
my father.

I sent you a letter
two months after
my miscarriage.

I wrote mother, the day you die
I will be a bastard to this world.
      Who will love me
         when you're gone?

Mother, I am so lonely. I think
hummingbirds hate me
& butterflies just drop by
out of pity.

But the crickets        they laugh
with their song       every time
                      I miss you.

# How to Avoid Relapse

Be loved by divine light. Not by the light in which men
see you. Let the cosmos glitter down star stuff. Feel
the big bang's ashes seep into your pores. Become
a union with the universe. Let your eyes shine
out the strength of lighthouses. Reel people
into you. Smother out the darkness
in them. Become a flame's flicker
forgive everyone before
you dies out.

# Scraped

Was it because I knocked a baby hummingbird
from its nest when I was seven? Was that wrong?

Did the angels snitch on me
when they saw how I forced
that tiny little thing to fly?

Did they tell God or was he already watching?
Did God forget I jumped a five-foot wall to save
the hummingbird from those boys?

Does he remember my scraped knees?
Does he think about the blood like I do?

Did he smile when I offered the baby hummingbird
to my mother as a gift? Or did he smile when mother
refused to cage the hummingbird and plopped it back
into its nest?

Why is it six months after my miscarriage I keep
dreaming hummingbird memory over and over?
Is this God's way of talking to me?

Does he think about the blood like I do?
Tell me, does he think about the blood
like I do?

Will December 1st be beautiful?
Will it snow somewhere?

When will hummingbirds teach me
how to fly backwards?

# Notes

Born to Electrify: The first line of the poem was taken from the third line of "The Girl with the Moon in her Heart" by Louise Emily Thomas.

With Hunger: Won a 1st place poetry award from the *River's Voice*, the annual literary journal of the Rio Hondo College campus community. It is comprised of original works from students, faculty, staff, and alumni along five genres: poetry, short story, memoir, one-act drama, and visual art.

Mujer de Hielo Autopsia: Inspired by the Parasite Eve video game and novel.

Amor en El Pueblo: For my grandparents.

# Acknowledgements

I would like to thank the following publications, where some of the poems in this collection can be found: *San Gabriel Valley Poetry Quarterly*, *River's Voice*, *Cadence Collective*, and *East Jasmine Review*.

Thank you Half Off Books for providing a space where I always feel welcomed. Also, thank you, Eric Morago. I wouldn't have met any of the people I love and cherish today if it wasn't for SHOUT! or workshop.

I would like to give a big thank you to Sarah Thursday and Nancy Lynée Woo. "Born to Electrify" would have not made its way out into the world without the help of these two fine ladies. Without their love, encouragement, and guidance, I would have never known dreams, even the smallest ones, can come true. I am so honored and thankful to represent Sadie Girl Press. I will forever be a Sadie Girl at heart.

I'd like to thank you, the reader, my parents, my Virgo, and my friends for their support. A warm thanks to the kind poets surrounding my life. It is a pleasure to know you. You all inspire me to blossom. Thank you for supporting me in my poetic endeavors. Without you, this journey would not have been possible.

## About the Author

Raquel Reyes-Lopez was born in 1994. She started writing poetry at 9 years old. When her singing instructor crushed her dreams of ever becoming a singer, she knew she could not express herself through singing, her voice would be heard through writing. She is a member of the Whittier Poetry Group and assistant editor of Cadence Collective. She has an addiction to tea. From green tea to white willow bark tea to Irish Moss tea, she will drink it. Aside from tea addiction, she loves collecting Tarot card decks. She enjoys reading books on dream symbolism, numerology, and herbalism. To tell Raquel you enjoyed reading her work, find her at facebook.com/contactraquelreyeslopez.
*Author portrait by Fernando Gallegos.*